And The Sun Still Dared To Shine

Peter Scheponik

 Mazo Publishers

And The Sun Still Dared To Shine
ISBN: 978-1-936778-99-7
Copyright © 2011

Cover Image
© Lorpic99 | Dreamstime.com

Published by:
Mazo Publishers
Website: www.mazopublishers.com
Email: cm@mazopublishers.com
Tel: 1-815-301-3559

Returning The Memory Of The Holocaust
To A World Too Ready To Forget

Preface

In November of 2000, famed poet Robert Hass delivered a brilliant lecture at Montgomery County Community College on the art of poetry and the poet's role in society. Among the many astute and salient points that Robert Hass made in his delivery was his identification of the poet as "the keeper of memories." Mr. Hass went on to suggest that the poet "will know what memory he or she was meant to keep." This knowing that Mr. Hass referred to would be revealed in the poet's own mind and heart through the process of personal reflection and self-discovery.

Sitting in the audience, contemplating Mr. Hass's definition, I began ruminating on my own journey as a poet. I had already published in a number of journals and had one collection under my bardic belt. At the time, I was between poetry projects, so my poetic nature provided fertile ground for the inspirational seeds Mr. Hass was casting my way. Sitting there, that night, I heard a voice from deep inside of me whisper: Remember the Holocaust.

I have always felt a deep connection to the Holocaust, from the first revelation of the walls of human bodies I witnessed in the historical footage shown in my high school French class. I remember as I watched that documentary, placing my head down on the desk and being deeply ashamed of being a member of a species capable of such unspeakable inhumanity. Years later, when my life's journey took me to middle school and junior high as a social studies teacher, I was appalled that the events of the Holocaust could be summarized in textbooks, reduced to a mere paragraph or two listing the human losses as over eleven million, six million of whom were Jews. I made it my quest to provide my students with a greater exposure to the truth of this watershed event that had changed the course of history and the heart of humanity forever. Thus, I became actively engaged in the study of Holocaust history and literature and keenly aware of contemporary trends of anti-Semitism and Holocaust denial.

Robert Hass's lecture rekindled my commitment to remembering the Holocaust and refocused my efforts in the way that I would remember. I decided that moment, at that lecture, that I would return to my research on the Holocaust and bring its memory back to a world that was too ready to forget. I decided to accomplish this through one of humanity's most intimate art forms – poetry. But the poetry I would write would be based on facts, based on actual lives and events. I wanted these poems to live and breathe in the hearts of the readers, to make them stop and see the reality of mankind's loss.

Navigating the sea of tragedy that constituted the Holocaust would be a daunting endeavor. Where would I begin? Whose stories would I tell? How would I end? These were questions that hung in the air above me like a trinity of hungry and haunting albatrosses. I hoisted the sails of inquiry and resolve, and with empathy as my compass guide, embarked on a journey that would lead me from the depths of collective suffering to the heights of individual heroism. This collection of poetry presents the reader with genocidal images of deprivation, deportation, and dehumanization. These poems allow the reader to peer through the slots of the transport boxcars and witness the horrific degradation that preceded the merciless torture and deaths of the millions who passed through the camps' gates. These verses narrate the traumatic losses of family and friends, of personal identity, of individual liberty, of human dignity, of physical necessities, of psychological stability, of spiritual security, and, ultimately, of life. Finally, these stanzas also reveal the indomitable spirit of endurance, the relentless capacity for hope amidst adversity, the inalienable need to love and be loved, and the irrepressible will to survive.

In the epic desolation of the Holocaust, enormity becomes anonymity. The sheer numbers of the victims and magnitude of their agony remains annihilating. When these poems decided to be born, I found myself confronted with the implausible task of trying to deliver what Lawrence Langer, in *Admitting the Holocaust*, so judiciously identified as the "unimaginable" (79). My purpose in writing this small volume is an attempt to remind all who enter these poems of their solemn and very human duty to remember.

And The Sun Still Dared To Shine

In the Country

Below a barn floor
an opening like a
grave dug for one
filled with two sisters
who lay side by side for months,
unspeakable twins
clinging to the gun
like the truth
their brother had
given them.

Should the Germans come
they were to shoot themselves,
first one, then the other,
to escape the camps
that were far worse
than the muscle cramps
from lack of movement
than the heat and darkness
of the humid earth or
the razor sharp bite
of rats' teeth
gnawing the tender flesh
of naked toes,
worse even than
when the water came,
rising to their chins
till they floated like pickles
in the belly of the salt barrel,
drowning in darkness.

Jabłko[1]

When the edict came
announcing death
to anyone aiding a Jew,
they brought her in,
fearing for their lives,
delivering the four-year-old girl
to the guard
who gave her an apple
asked her her name
vowed to find
the mother who
abandoned her child,
then turned as
the young girl
started to eat
and fired the shot
into her head,
blood soaking
the ringlets of
her curls, changing their color
from blonde to red,
as she dropped
to the earth
like fruit from the bough,
the apple
turning round
and round.

[1] Apple

Truth

Sometimes
they lured
them out of
hiding with
bread promises
spread before them,
like manna
in the desert
of starvation
so that they
came willingly
to the cattle cars,
the linings
of their stomachs
already fusing,
their throats
cut with pain.

It was a time
when bread
was the only truth.

Boxcar Hell I

No light
no air
no water
for days
so that some
licked the tears
from sweating bodies
or drank
their own urine,
carefully cupping
the saving flow
in their own hands
raising the sordid hope
like a golden promise
to cracked lips and
parched throats,
as if answering
a higher call,
both ancient and sacred,
the need to hold on,
the duty to survive.

Boxcar Hell II

Locked in darkness
movement becomes
memory
like house and job
food and water
in the thick black
square of hell
on wheels,
journey of the damned
where the dead
tell stories
to the dead,
where faith and hope
swim in excrement.

Tainted Nature

The floodlights
bathe the platform
in merciless white stupor
as guards direct
right, left,
life, death,
the hopeless lines
pouring from cattle car mouths.
A screaming child
hauled to the left,
howls for its mother
as a grinning guard
gives the woman her chance to go,
accompany her offspring
into the flames.

In a moment
pregnant with impossibilities,
the mother wife daughter
woman child blind instinct to live,
refuses to follow.

The Discovery

When she discovers
that women with children
are moving toward
the chimney
spewing clouds of
smoke that smells like death,
she smiles at her daughter
gathers her grandchild
in her arms,
close to her heart,
and rocks the way
she danced her daughter
to sleep
in the night,
moving away
from nightmares,
the love within her
burning.
It is an act of
hope in hopelessness,
this grandmother
who carries her grandchild
into the gas,
into the flames,
this mother
who would save
her own daughter.

Salon

Upon heartless chairs
in a hopeless room
the staggered women sat,
hair falling
like souls into
endless sacks.
Five cuts cleaned a head,
left the body breathing,
the woman, inside, dead
as the heaping strands
bagged and bound and
shipped away
in this mattress and slipper industry.

The Shearing

In the barber's den,
the lines of the naked
stood in waiting
like sheep at the shearer's,
the hair shorn by the
sharp teeth of blades,
red-tipped razors
that bit the flesh edges
as the silken tresses
fell and lay
helpless as the victims
who stood and turned,
arms raised
legs spread
stripped of their hair
the way they were stripped of
their luggage
their clothes
their humanity
removed
a layer at a time
till all that remained
were the nicked and bleeding bodies,
waiting for the gas.

Sorting

In an area for
sorting,
young from old
men from women
husbands from wives
parents from children
meaning from lives
souls from bodies
of those who died
in gas chambers,
he separated the separated,
clothing from victims,
mindlessly sorting
shirts from blouses
skirts from trousers
coats from shawls
until he held in
his own hands
his own brother:
a small pile
of clothes and pictures.

The Moment

When he dropped
the pile of clothing
to gather his young son
into his arms,
he let go of death
to embrace life,
suspending hell.
For a moment,
everything stopped:
the endless trains,
the hopeless lines,
the separation,
the tearing off clothing,
the terror in eyes,
the naked bodies
driven dumbstruck
to gaseous deaths.
Until the guards
saw the pair,
and a father
sent his son
to shower.

The Offering

When she pulled away from her mother
and offered herself
to the one collecting clothes, her garments
at her feet in a meaningless heap,
she was offering him her whole body
with the force of her whole soul,
her fingertips softly kissing her young flesh,
hungry for love
hungry for life,
the desire to live, strong as her sobs
that were greeted by guards who took it all,
breaking her like little sticks,
while he rushed away in darkness,
facedeep in cotton folds.

Shoes

He has hopes of
finding her,
his young wife
separated at
the ramp,
she to the left,
he to the right,
their boy taken
in the furious night
of fierce tongues
licking the black sky
and smoke belching
from the roaring throat
of the chimney soaring
while somewhere below
in a sealed room
the bodies lay
in a mass of blue flesh,
tangled and barbed
like wire.

Weeks later,
shaved, striped, and numbered,
he finds her
in a mountain of despair,
all that's left,
a neatly tied pair,
piled with hundreds of others,
shoes so carefully arranged
that not a single one was lost.

Baby Strollers

In the middle of hell,
the baby strollers rolled
their precious cargo
of jewels and cash,
watches and bonds,
the looted lives
of the damned.
The infants,
already slag on
the chimney's
throat.

Baths

Denuded and deranged
hope and hopelessness
mixed with Zyklon B and air
terror and moans
moving in madness
through minutes without end
till all that remained
in the center of the room
was a pyramid of blue flesh
reaching the concrete ceiling
where their wild climb
clawed its mark
in stains of blood red testimony.

Children of the Gas

The very young, three to five year olds,
slipped between the spaces
of the twisted dead,
finding just enough air
among the bodies so tightly packed
that the gas couldn't reach
them there, to kill them,
so it left them instead,
glazed over in an agony
of cataract eyes
closed with the memory of
the final surge toward the ceiling,
one body climbing over the other
in the final race for air,
in a vacuum of deafened ears
filled with the final screams and
gasps of suffocation,
the last sounds they'd ever hear,
unable to share their story,
sing their song of sorrow,
because their vocal chords
were taut as the bodies of
the tangled dead that were
pulled apart with grappling hooks,
revealing these babes
whose second chances were
grasped like little ankles
in SS fists and smashed
like small skulls against the bleeding walls.

Roll Call

In the icy cold
of winter wind
they stood for hours,
numbed into numbers.
Behind them,
the ovens' thawing roar,
above them,
the warmth of human smoke.

Love Photos

When they ordered him to undress,
he shed his clothing like his life
falling into the heap of
other shed lives,
rising like a mountain that
would match the mountains of
muscle and blood
skin and bones
starved and stacked
and ready for burning.

In his arms he held his shoes,
the pictures of his family
wrapped in paper, stuffed inside,
hidden like Jews in
basements and attics,
forests and barns.

Later when they gave him
his cap and stripes,
fed him crust bread and
black water coffee,
forced him to labor
and attend the endless roll calls,
he'd stand in the courtyard for hours,
stripped of hope and dignity,
the sole of his foot
kissing the faces of those photographs
in the silent defiance of love.

Cold Night at Mauthausen

One winter night,
two hundred
were herded
into a frigid room
and given blankets
soaked in ice water,
with their own hands
they were forced to wrap themselves
in death,
their souls slowly rising
to the surface,
glistening like ice
on winter branches.

Protocol for the Living

He moans,
his swollen face
an agony of infection,
the urine-soaked cloth
unable to contain
the noise of his pain
permeating the barrack,
stealing sleep,
the second bread in Hell,
until they came,
some of his own,
took him quietly
to a corner,
leaned on his legs,
put the pillow to his
face and pressed
their waking nightmare
to an end.

Die Muss Spazieren[2]

After the fumigation
to protect the SS from typhus,
the inmates carried their dead vermin
like a memory of being eaten alive,
their skin
once crawling with countless mouths
feeding off their flesh the way
the guards fed off their suffering
moment by moment
hour by hour
devouring inside and out
till meeting in the middle of
inexorable hunger,
where the offer of an extra bowl of broth
became both blessing and hope
for the one who could find a living louse,
who could slog through
the blood and excrement
behind the barracks,

digging for the parasite promise,
that would bring the chance to eat.

[2] *It has to walk.*

The Mark of Cane

Twenty-five lashes with the cane,
the pants pulled down,
head thrust deeply into the
filled well of the latrine
so that every scream
was drowned
in excrement,
survival consisting
of bleeding buttocks
broken as spirits
and a head and face
stained with shame
that couldn't be wiped away.

Witness I

Slowly they shoveled,
sprinkling the sand
which turned to red sugar
when it covered the blood
running from holes
in the backs of heads,
forming a river that ran red
from the black wall
where the chosen stood
hearing the shots
seeing their brothers fall
one by one,
an agony of waiting,
while the shovels
endlessly turned,
stirring black terror with red death
in a mixture of blood and sand.

Witness II

After the last of the bullets flew,
the last of the bodies fell
for the day,
silence swallowed all
but the quiet roll
of blood through sand
and the steady buzz of flies.

The Ritual

In stolen moments,
precious as crusts
of hardened bread
or the savored sips
of water-thin broth,
the shorn women sat,
their kerchief rags
resting on their knees
silent as the destiny
fallen upon their heads
bowed, as if in prayer,
while they passed
the piece of comb,
smuggled like a
Davidic psalm
from hand to hand,
head to head
moving truth like teeth
through the half inch of
hair that dared to grow
in a place of darkness,
the lice dropping into their laps,
falling like tiny ashes.

Story of Water

And when the
flood waters came,
the amniotic fluid
bursting forth
like a spring of life
in a place of death,
her friend was told
by the guard
to boil water,
as the young mother pushed
and screamed,
ripped and bled,
squeezing the new life,
wet with promises,
through her dry soul,
like the first rays of sunlight
piercing the darkness.
How could she imagine,
bathed in sweat and broken capillaries,
that when the cord was cut,
the flow of blood tied,

her child's first cries
would be drowned
in the hiss of
boiling water.

Afterlife

It was when he
closed his eyes
as the guard
raised his arm
and aimed the gun
that the wooden plank
whacked from behind
and everything went black,
blacker than the swastikas
and boxcar journeys,
blacker than the night sky
against the chimney's
sanguine flare,
a sinking blackness that
seemed like death,
swallowing what was left,
salvation of unconsciousness,
until he opened his eyes
to SS sneers that the afterlife
belonged to the Fatherland
and the bullet to his head.

Beast of the Pit

In the belly of the pit,
the iron beast bent,
jurassic jaws
snapped and clenched
the tangled mass of
human flesh,
tearing chunks
with metal teeth
that tightly locked,
bursting skin
and breaking bone,
the pieces dropping,
heads and hands
on legs and arms,
bits of food
from slavering jaws,
a human pile
glistering with blood.

In Mannequin Pieces

On the table
she rests,
hollow torso
of the dead:
two arms and
two breasts
in stiff repose,
a woman
unmade
with scalpel hate,
her body
opened and emptied
as if taking her life
were not enough,
the cavity of her chest
scraped clean,
the sharp edges
digging for her soul.

Child's Play

And the flames
from the crematoria
leapt from the ovens and into
the hearts and minds
of the children
dancing like
dreams of death
they could not understand
but would
as they played
with the small pit
they dug with
their own hands
dropping stones
like bodies into
its hungry mouth
and screaming—
innocently practicing
for the day they would
enter the flames.

Bread from Heaven

When the air raid struck the camp,
heaping death the way
they were forced to shovel dirt
into the faces of the still living,
they ran for shelter, two boys,
one with bread
one with hunger,
crouched in corners
curled under bunks,
the harsh wooden planks of pain
suddenly warm dreams of shelter
maternal as arms
in darkness,
safety from explosions and flames,
the sharp clods of shrapnel earth.

When the planes left
and the smoke cleared,
the one with bread lay dead,
his deep eyes staring at
the one with hunger,
stuffing the hardened morsels
into his shocked, dry throat,
gorging himself with life,
with this last chance to eat.

Fertig[3]

In a place of starvation,
a piece of bread
becomes life.
So when
he asked his
bunk mate
to guard his morsel,
and his closest
friend guarded it
with the tabernacle
of his body,
immersing that
bread of life into
the full power
of his hunger,
no apology
was enough,
no promise of a
return ration
that afternoon
would suffice,
only a plank of wood
against the throat
that had swallowed the food
and the final stomp
of the guard's heavy heel
would do.

[3] *Finished!*

Helena's Friend

She awakened one morning
in the freezing cold,
bare as winter branches,
stiff with frigid air,
next to her
her foot and some of her leg,
frozen like her
life broken off,
like her soul
blocked out
in a place of
cold horror
and dry ice hearts.

She clung to herself,
begging a friend
to help with the burial,
to save some part
of her from harm.

Gornisht[4]

After the English bombing,
the inmates rummage,
sifting through rubble,
looking for life,
finding more death
in the ruptured
layers of hell
where they shuffle,
staggered by hunger,
wracked with pain,
their stomachs
turned cannibal
dissolving themselves,
too long since the
last mouthful of cheese,
the sawdust crust of bread,
the sliced translucence of wurst.

Amidst the debris,
a severed hand,
crushed between bricks and cinder,
its flesh palm belly, a raw roast,
divided among five
who cut and swallow
the fruits of their labor.

[4] *Nothing at all*

Remnants of the Civilized

At Radom
they led them,
thirty Jews,
from the place
where they molded
guns, fashioned the
very bullets that
would be used to
fire into their
helpless bodies
that would fall into
the hopeless graves
they had dug with
their own hands,
hard labor of
their own muscles
toiling toward death,
their own — civilization's.
They were herded
into the locked room
in the bowels of the earth,
no windows, no water,
no place to relieve themselves,
to find relief from the indignity
flooding their lives.
In the darkness,
the men used
pieces of string
to stop the urine's flow.

Confession

There was a private room
for the ones who wouldn't confess,
who wouldn't betray,
delivering themselves or their cellmates
over into SS hands.
For crimes of holding onto humanity,
they were forced to hold
onto their scrotums,
lower the victim testicles
into the vat of icy water
until the sack contracted with cold
turned red, then purple,
next, the scalding vat
that drew the testes back to earth,
quick thaw burning flesh gone raw,
bright red with blisters,
hot, cold, then hot again,
the whole time cradling their manhood
with trembling fingers
until iodine poured into open wounds
like hot grease into the ruptured burn.
How they screamed and howled
in mourning and pain,
the price of their human dignity.
How they learned, on bended knees,
to confess.

The Hooks I

Sometimes,
just for their pleasure,
the SS guards
would take
the inmates,
draw their captive arms
behind their hostage backs,
fettering them tightly
with cords and hate,
the ropes cutting off
the circulation,
the blood burning in
the crushed veins
like the lust throbbing
in SS groins
as they hung the victims
from the hooks,
by their bound arms,
their feet dangling freely
in the air
as the shoulder joints
would slowly tear
from their sockets,
sinews and tendons
pulled out like roots.
In the agony of affliction
they would howl for hours.

The Hooks II

Other times,
victims were hung,
slowly strangled,
on the hooks
in the crematorium
whose black brick
chimney was slagged with
roasted flesh,
blackened with blood
crusting its mortared throat,
the dust of bones like
death in the air,
choking last breaths
of the dying as the
guards tightened
the cords around
their victims' throats
the way one twists
the soaked rag
lifted from the bucket,
slowly wringing
the last drops.

Puppenjungen[5]

Some were fifteen,
some younger,
food for starving men
hungry for starving boys
they lured with bits of meat,
with swallows of milk
they gave them
to eat,
to be eaten,
these youths who
became kindling
to feed the fires.

[5] *Doll boys*

Eat and Sleep

Curled in comfortable quarters,
the guard dogs slept,
black muzzles put away
like weapons
tucked in warm fur,
their well-fed bodies
filled with "oats" and "potatoes,"
"meat" and "milk,"
dreaming barbed wire dreams,
while inmates
crammed on wooden planks
lined the walls with
hunger nightmares of
sharp white teeth
tearing canvas flesh
over wooden bones
their stomachs,
writhing night and day,
dissolving inside out
until they lay
on human mounds,
where bloated rats
covered countless faces
with hairless tails
and bright red teeth,
consuming the evidence
while the whole world slept.

And the Stones, too, Shall Bleed

In a narrow hallway,
they were forced to
hop until hunger
and weakness
drew them to their
knees, dropped them
on their sides.
Like felled husks
they lay,
their shrivelled forms
crunching
under SS heels
that stomped on noses
and dug into ears,
drawing blood
from a dry bed
of stones.

The Drain

After they were shot,
one by one
in eye witness order,
the gun just inches
from the back of the neck,
they were brought
to the drain,
the opening of the
pipe almost kissing
the opening of the flesh
at the base of the skull,
the blood of the body
almost warming
the throat of the
cold metal pipe.

When the last drops fell
in bright red tears,
the bodies were stacked,
one on the other,
like loaves on the rack
to cool.

LiLi's Love Letter

And when they seized her,
she was just eighteen,
her crime,
a letter she guarded
like her life,
the memory of love
in a place where love
was forbidden
like food and water,
clothing and rest.
They stood her naked
against the wall,
ordered the rifles raised,
and fired a volley of
bitter clicks from empty barrels,
their intent to torture
before they shot,
an endless cycle
of tearful cringing
and laughing guards
until she knelt and
begged to die.

They pitied her
with bullets.

Catalepsy

At the stripping place,
he ran from sorting room
to loading dock,
bundling the clothes,
building the hopeless piles
a shirt, a coat, a dress at a time,
until he was transferred,
told to climb the mountains of bodies
and mine the cavernous mouths for gold.

He stood there
paralyzed,
the cold metal pliers,
hanging from his hand.

Winter Warmth

In the biting cold,
children were put
to the cart,
dragging ashes
heaped like death,
mothers, fathers,
sisters, brothers,
flaky remains
like dirty snow that
small hands scattered
on icy roads to
keep the flow of SS troops
from slipping.
When their work was done,
if the gassing rooms
were empty,
they were invited in
to escape the cold,
Rachael's children,
who were no more,
warming themselves
with death.

Accident

When the guard
spotted him
trying to hide
his guilt,
a single piece of wood
miscut,
he grabbed the prisoner,
forced his terrified wrist
to the saw
blade screaming
through sinew and bone.

Careening about the room,
crazed with shock,
glazed with blood,
the wild inmate died,
the whole time,
trying to press back into place,
his severed hand.

Children of Zamosc

When they led the children
to the room and
told them to undress,
they responded with
naked innocence.
When they directed them
to stand or sit,
they obeyed,
eyes wide with
fear and trust,
raising their left arms
high as they were told,
exposing their fragile ribs,
beating hearts,
perfect targets
for the hypodermic thrust,
and phenolic kiss,
their cries of acid death
unheard
as they dropped,
their own mouths covered
with their tiny arms,
just as they'd been told.

The Dolls

Like the little bodies
heaped in the pit
rigid with death,
the mute dolls lie,
wide-eyed
opened-mouthed
piled high,
their little arms and legs
outstretched.
But the dolls
have hair and
baby fat happiness
covering their small
plastic bones –
the dolls still have clothes.

Isaac the Strong[6]

For one,
survival meant
drowning,
taking inmates
into the
water-filled pit,
with his own hands,
with his own great strength,
a blinded Samson,
holding their heads
below the muddy waters
until the last bubbles
broke in silence,
his own people
lost in a backward
exodus,
overwhelmed by a sea of blood,
until
under the water,
he saw his own father,
and his hands
let go, his strength
toppling like
Philistine pillars,
his screams of madness,
silenced only
by SS guns.

[6] *Directly taken from the testimony of survivor Josef Kral*

Divine Mercy

On command,
the dog trained to chew
the genitals of Jewish men
would lunge,
cutting a covenant of death
for those who moved too slowly
or failed to obey.

For these,
a bullet to the head
was mercy.

The Game

For some,
killing became a game,
fifty a day,
on a pile of sand
at the finish line,
the guards' black boots
and cruel command:
Strip! Run! Kneel! Bow!

The prize: no beating before you died.

Lechaim[7] Andreas Rappaport

In the cell,
waiting for his death,
he raked
his own flesh,
digging the nails deeply
into his skin
to bring forth his life,
the blood within
him shed,
carefully writing,
with fingertips,
his name and age
on the wall:
"Andreas Rappaport –
lived sixteen years,"[8]
as if inscribing his name
in the book of life.

[7] *To life*
[8] *Quoted from the testimony of survivor Josef Gluck*

Clepsydra[9]

When the young boy
turned his wounded face,
looked into his father's eyes,
asked him if he were
marked for death,
fear and love pressed the two
together like hands in prayer.
In the night,
in the cell,
in despair,
the father propped the box
looped the belts
about their necks
then around the beam,
first his son,
then himself,
their only hope to escape
the biting shovels,
the burning trenches.

[9] Marked for death

The Pact

With darkness came
the rasp of wood,
as the box was pushed,
like the sound of a
throat being cleared,
the stretch of the belt
full weight of gravity
pulling the body in the
black thrash of air
between feet and floor,
humanity lost
regained in darkness.
This was choice.

Nightwatch

At night
in the cellblock
in the darkness
thick with death,
one walked with
arms outstretched,
like the blind
feeling their way
between the
hanging bodies.

The Lost One

Among the bodies
layered like logs,
arms and legs
rigid with death,
eyes vacant as
ghettos drained
to pack the
black box
cattle cars
of endless trains
that gorged
the gas rooms,
stuffed the ovens
till their black throats
split with blood,
a little girl
crawled and curled
between dead limbs,
like a wounded cat
waiting to die.

Ash Wednesday

Clouds of smoke
swallowed the sky
as the open pit flamed
like the mouth of hell,
bodies bursting,
fat sizzling into
furrowed drains,
the SS joking about
potatoes burning,
the screaming children
thrown in alive.

Interrogation

On a bar between two tables,
they would beat them to a spin,
iron rod between elbows
and behind the knees,
bull-whipping them
till their wills ran like blood
over handcuffed wrists,
and they'd finally give in,
their screams,
muffled in masks.

Consummation I

In a compound
ankle deep with blood,
they lay in red repose,
the bodies of women,
whose beauty
death had left untouched,
marred only by knives
that had severed the breasts
and blades that had
sliced the thighs.

Consummation II

From the trenches
around the flaming pit,
where melted fat ran
like colorless blood,
they scooped the glycerin,
thick and hot,
to baste the burning bodies.

Lost and Found

And there were times
in the fury of
final solution,
from a pile of clothing,
a child emerged,
lost or hidden,
delivered into SS arms,
one more purged
with bullet swiftness.

Red Sky over Auschwitz

And when the endless bodies
fed into the ground
rotted and swelled,
the earth, sick with murder,
vomited thick red sludge
of flesh and blood,
made a leprosy of the land
and a poison of the water
so that even the fish
began to die.
So they gave the order
to exhume the dead,
burn the remains,
as if fire could
cleanse the guilt,
consume the shame
of ovens heated,
pits set aflame.
At night the sky
was turned to blood.

Lechaim II

As he stood there,
platzjude,[10]
waiting for her clothing,
watching her undress,
the old woman, weary,
certain of her death,
questioned him
about the others,
the men,
sent the other way.
In that moment
of silence,
eternal as truth,
they stood there,
he with nothing to say,
she kissing his hand
bade him live,
told that son of Abraham
to "Go on!"[11]

[10] Jews of the square who sorted the confiscated belongings of the concentration camp prisoners
[11] Quoted from the testimony of survivor Meir Berliner

The Pit

In the inferno of the pit,
the bodies seemed to live again.
Melting faces moved to tears
of fat which seared
the writhing skin
that thinned and swelled,
shrank and tore from
smoking bones
in death sweat agony.
The rounded stomach of a mother to be
broke like a dam
in amniotic hiss
as the fetus burst forth,
ascending in a leap of flames.

Love's Mockery

On their way to the fires,
some of the women were slit,
blade in the stomach,
blood and bowel
slipping to the floor,
while men were forced
by laughing guards
to mount and ride
the gutted dead.

Burial

Four dying
to drag
one dead
to the ragged edge
of the open trench
where the bodies lay
rigid with lime.

Camp Games

For fun,
the guards
would toss
the victim's cap
across the
death zone line
then order
the prisoner
to go and
fetch it
like a dog
after stick or bone.
They would
order the
victim to fetch
his own death,
his only chance,
a prayer for pity,
his only hope,
some kindness
in hell.
The only gift of
mercy ever given
came wrapped in
blood and gunfire.

Bread of Life

Sometimes,
a slice of bread
had to last
for days,
one slice
to quell the
burning hunger
that steadily
consumed
the insides
of bodies,
the way
the ovens
consumed
the outsides.
Honor and
hope dissolved
in gastric acids,
souls stuck to
stomach linings,
and throats swelled shut
so that even prayers
could not get through.
In the dark,
sons ate the bread
of their dying fathers.

Animal Warmth

While they froze
in the winter wind,
thin layer
of rag stripes
gaping over thin layer
of skin draping
over hollow bones,
the SS dogs,
well-fed,
prowled in animal warmth,
clothed in coats blazoned
with Nazi power,
coats made of human hair.

Desolation I

In that place,
the only light
was blood red
tongues of flame
making a desert of
a fertile land
so that the women
even ceased to bleed.

These Bones Will Shout

And when the
hungry flames
finished
what the
hunger of hate
had begun,
the great
mountains of
calcified matter
screamed
white vengeance
from their
smoked marrow hearts
until they
took the bones,
ground them
like white shale
for roads,
paving the way
for the fatherland,
lining the trenches
of latrines.

Sterilization

Forcing the young men
to hand over their manhood,
the way they handed over
their possessions, their hope, their names,
the doctors used X-rays,
waiting,
watching the testes descend,
making sure they weren't
hiding in attic groins.
Later, to be certain
they had murdered Jesse's root,
the way others had
murdered Rachael's children,
they devised a metal crank
to press the prostrate
with mechanized hate.
Two turns in the anus
and the ejaculate came,
flowing like milk and honey.

No Choice

At times,
the earth would move,
the dark brown loam
ripple as if the ground
itself were shivering,
a tingle running up
its spine,
the arms and legs
of those still alive,
covered with dirt
shoveled by victims
covering victims,
the clods of earth
muffling the moans,
drinking the tears
of a mother
begging her son
not to bury her alive.

Sisterhood of the Bullet

In seconds,
the red dot appeared,
as if a
butterfly of blood
had landed
on her forehead,
spread its crimson wings
which ran like tears
down the cheeks
of each
of the women
lined up,
face to back,
as they dropped,
one, after the other,
the way the stalks
of corn fall
to the thresher's slash,
until the single bullet exited,
tiny wet burst,
from the back
of the last woman's head,
leaving her toppled,
like all the rest—dead,
sisterhood of the bullet.

Punishment

The weight of
the rock presses
directly upon
the child's head,
crushing the
vertebrae in
the small
neck struggling
to stay straight
as the little
arms, outstretched,
quivered from
the dense pull
of the bricks—
one in each hand,
while the tender knees
ached on the
courtyard grit,
in the hot sun,
kneeling for hours,
for eating a crust of bread
during roll call.

Because

Because she cried
when they took her home,
her family, her child, her hair;
the SS matron took her coat,
the one thing she had left,
leaving her only winter air
to comfort her in her mourning.

Furnace of life

It began as a
small ring,
five or six men
against the damp
and cold,
then spread like
revelation,
fire spark of
survival
in hundreds of
broken bodies
who came
and joined
swayed and sang
for hours,
a prayer of
physical union.

In the center of
the huddled mass,
a circle of human heat
warmed like faith
and spread like life,
against the oven mouths
that roared with endless death.

Vengeance

In a room
piled with the
clothes of those
already gassed,
with the corpses stacked
like logs for the
white hot mouths
that burned night and day,
turned bodies to smoke,
souls to ashes,
some fought back.
Rebel wills
turned to knives,
surrounded the guard
with silver blades
whose rage red edges
sharp as despair
slipped in and out
like sanity
or glistening words
of angry prayers:

"for my father,
for my brother,
and for everybody you killed."[12]

[12] *These words were taken from the testimony of survivor Chaim E.*
Sobibor.

Still

And as the trains spilled their cargo,
dumbstruck,
onto the ramps
snarling with dogs
snapping with whips
shouting with orders
from black boot guards
holding loaded guns,
the lines parted
left from right,
men from women
mothers from children
old from young
sick from healthy
belongings from passengers
living from dead
clothing from bodies
gas from showerheads
breath from lungs
flames from flames
flesh from bones
smoke from chimneys
hope from hearts
ash from air.

And the sun still dared to shine,
pressing melted gold fingers
through crematory clouds,
while birds sang their hallowed tunes aloud
for those who could bear to listen.

References

1.) The historical context of "In the Country" is based on testimony presented in Holocaust Testimonies: The Ruins of Memory, by Lawrence L. Langer (10-11).

2.) The historical context of "Jabtko" is based on testimony presented in Witness: Voices from the Holocaust, edited by Joshua M. Greene and Shiva Kumar (70-71).

3.) The historical context of "Truth" is based on testimony presented in Witnesses to the Holocaust, edited by Rhoda G. Lewin (80).

4.) The historical context of "Box Car Hell I" is based on testimony presented in Daily Life During the Holocaust, written by Eve Nussbaum Soumerai and Carol D. Schulz (171-172).

5.) The historical context of "Box Car Hell II" is based on testimony presented in Daily Life During the Holocaust, by Eva Nussbaum Soumerai and Carol D. Schultz (171).

6.) The historical context of "Tainted Nature" is based on testimony presented in Holocaust Testimonies: The Ruins of Memory, by Lawrence L. Langer (12).

7.) The historical context of "The Discovery" is based on testimony presented in Witnesses to the Holocaust, edited by Rhoda G. Lewin (6).

8.) The historical context of "Salon" is based on testimony presented in Treblinka, written by Jean-Francois Steiner, Translated by Helen Weaver (166).

9.) The historical context of "The Shearing" is based on testimony presented in Witness: Voices from the Holocaust, edited by Joshua M. Greene and Shiva Kumar (120).

10.) The historical context of "Sorting" is based on testimony presented in Witness: Voices from the Holocaust, edited by Joshua M. Greene and Shiva Kumar (131).

11.) The historical context of "The Moment" is based on testimony presented in Treblinka, written by Jean-Francois Steiner, Translated by Helen Weaver (60-61).

12.) The historical context of "The Offering" is based on testimony presented in Treblinka, written by Jean-Francois Steiner, Translated by Helen Weaver (76-78).

13.) The historical context of "Shoes" is based on testimony presented in Auschwitz, written by Bernard Naumann, translated by Jean Steinberg (272).

14.) The historical context of "Baby Strollers" is based on testimony presented in Witnesses to the Holocaust, edited by Rhoda G. Lewin (46).

15.) The historical context of "Baths" is based on testimony presented in Inside the Concentration Camps: Eyewitness Accounts in Hitler's Death Camps, compiled by Eugene Aroneanu, translated by Thomas Whissen (128-130).

16.) The historical context of "Children of the Gas" is based on testimony presented in The Buchenwald Report, translated and edited by David A. Hackett (350, 353).

17.) The historical context of "Roll Call" is based on testimony presented in Witnesses to the Holocaust, edited by Rhoda G. Lewin (17).

18.) The historical context of "Love Photos" is based on testimony presented in Witnesses to the Holocaust, edited by Rhoda G. Lewin (106).

19.) The historical context of "Cold Night at Mauthausen" is based on testimony presented in Holocaust Testimonies: The Ruins of Memory, by Lawrence L. Langer (28).

20.) The historical context of "Protocol for the Living" is based on testimony presented in Holocaust Testimonies: The Ruins of Memory, by Lawrence L. Langer (87).

21.) The historical context of "Die Muss Spazieren" is based on testimony presented in Holocaust Testimonies: The Ruins of Memory, by Lawrence L. Langer (115-116).

22.) The historical context of "The Mark of Cane" is based on testimony presented in The Buchenwald Report, translated and edited by David A. Hackett (75, 197).

23.) The historical context of "Witness I" is based on testimony presented in Auschwitz, written by Bernard Naumann, translated by Jean Steinberg (167-68).

24.) The historical context of "Witness II" is based on testimony presented in Auschwitz, written by Bernard Naumann, translated by Jean Steinberg (167-68).

25.) The historical context of "The Ritual" is based on testimony presented in Witness: Voices from the Holocaust, edited by Joshua M. Greene and Shiva Kumar (137).

26.) The historical context of "Story of Water" is based on testimony presented in Holocaust Testimonies: The Ruins of Memory, by Lawrence L. Langer (123).

27.) The historical context of "AfterLife" is based on testimony presented in Inside the Concentration Camps: Eyewitness Accounts in Hitler's Death Camps, compiled by Eugene Aroneanu, translated by Thomas Whissen (37).

28.) The historical context of "Beast of the Pit" is based on testimony presented in Treblinka, written by Jean-Francois Steiner, Translated by Helen Weaver (278).

29.) The historical context of "In Mannequin Pieces" is based on testimony presented in Inside the Concentration Camps: Eyewitness Accounts in Hitler's Death Camps, compiled by Eugene Aroneanu, translated by Thomas Whissen (based on picture in chap. 8).

30.) The historical context of "Child's Play" is based on testimony presented in The Murders at Bullenhuser Damm: The SS Doctor and the Children, written by Gunther Schwarberg, translated by Erna Baber Rosenfeld with Alvin H. Rosenfeld (16).

31.) The historical context of "Bread from Heaven" is based on testimony presented in Holocaust Testimonies: The Ruins of Memory, by Lawrence L. Langer (168).

32.) The historical context of "Fertig" is based on testimony presented in Holocaust Testimonies: The Ruins of Memory, by Lawrence L. Langer (27).

33.) The historical context of "Helena's Friend" is based on testimony presented in Holocaust Testimonies: The Ruins of Memory, by Lawrence L. Langer (100).

34.) The historical context of "Gornisht" is based on testimony presented in Holocaust Testimonies: The Ruins of Memory, by Lawrence L. Langer (117).

35.) The historical context of "Remnants of the Civilized" is based on testimony presented in Holocaust Testimonies: The Ruins of Memory, by Lawrence L. Langer (113).

36.) The historical context of "Confession" is based on testimony presented in The Buchenwald Report, translated and edited by David A. Hackett (204).

37.) The historical context of "The Hooks I" is based on testimony presented in The Buchenwald Report, translated and edited by David A. Hackett (154).

38.) The historical context of "The Hooks II" is based on testimony presented in The Buchenwald Report, translated and edited by David A. Hackett (154).

39.) The historical context of "Puppenjungen" is based on testimony presented in The Buchenwald Report, translated and edited by David A. Hackett (74).

40.) The historical context of "Eat and Sleep" is based on testimony presented in The Buchenwald Report, translated and edited by David A. Hackett (149) and from testimony presented in Witness: Voices from the Holocaust, edited by

Joshua M. Greene and Shiva Kumar (175).

41.) The historical context of "And the Stones, too, Shall Bleed" is based on testimony presented in The Buchenwald Report, translated and edited by David A. Hackett (197).

42.) The historical context of "The Drain" is based on testimony presented in Auschwitz, written by Bernard Naumann, translated by Jean Steinberg (135).

43.) The historical context of "LiLi's Love Letter" is based on testimony presented in Auschwitz, written by Bernard Naumann, translated by Jean Steinberg (130).

44.) The historical context of "Catalepsy" is based on testimony presented in Treblinka, written by Jean-Francois Steiner, Translated by Helen Weaver (63-64).

45.) The historical context of "Winter Warmth" is based on testimony presented in Auschwitz, written by Bernard Naumann, translated by Jean Steinberg (283).

46.) The historical context of "Accident" is based on testimony presented in Witness: Voices from the Holocaust, edited by Joshua M. Greene and Shiva Kumar (157).

47.) The historical context of "Children of Zamosc" is based on testimony presented in Auschwitz, written by Bernard Naumann, translated by Jean Steinberg (138).

48.) The historical context of "The Dolls" is based on testimony presented in Inside the Concentration Camps: Eyewitness Accounts in Hitler's Death Camps, compiled by Eugene Aroneanu, translated by Thomas Whissen (based on picture in chap. 10).

49.) The historical context of "Isaac the Strong" is based on testimony presented in Auschwitz, written by Bernard Naumann, translated by Jean Steinberg (146).

50.) The historical context of "Divine Mercy" is based on testimony presented in Treblinka, written by Jean-Francois Steiner, Translated by Helen Weaver (127).

51.) The historical context of "The Game" is based on testimony presented in Treblinka, written by Jean-Francois Steiner, Translated by Helen Weaver (316).

52.) The historical context of "Lechaim, Andreas Rappaport" is based on testimony presented in Auschwitz, written by Bernard Naumann, translated by Jean Steinberg (218).

53.) The historical context of "Clepsydra" is based on testimony presented in

Treblinka, written by Jean-Francois Steiner, Translated by Helen Weaver (76-80).

54.) The historical context of "The Pact" is based on testimony presented in Treblinka, written by Jean-Francois Steiner, Translated by Helen Weaver (78).

55.) The historical context of "Nightwatch" is based on testimony presented in Treblinka, written by Jean-Francois Steiner, Translated by Helen Weaver (81).

56.) The historical context of "The Lost One" is based on testimony presented in Auschwitz, written by Bernard Naumann, translated by Jean Steinberg (132).

57.) The historical context of "Ash Wednesday" is based on testimony presented in Auschwitz, written by Bernard Naumann, translated by Jean Steinberg (355).

58.) The historical context of "Interrogation" is based on testimony presented in Auschwitz, written by Bernard Naumann, translated by Jean Steinberg (169-170).

59.) The historical context of "Consummation I" is based on testimony presented in Auschwitz, written by Bernard Naumann, translated by Jean Steinberg (271).

60.) The historical context of "Consummation II" is based on testimony presented in Auschwitz, written by Bernard Naumann, translated by Jean Steinberg (267).

61.) The historical context of "Lost and Found" is based on testimony presented in Auschwitz, written by Bernard Naumann, translated by Jean Steinberg (180).

62.) The historical context of "Red Sky over Auschwitz" is based on testimony presented in Auschwitz, written by Bernard Naumann, translated by Jean Steinberg (173-174).

63.) The historical context of "Lechaim II" is based on testimony presented in Treblinka, written by Jean-Francois Steiner, Translated by Helen Weaver (73-74).

64.) The historical context of "The Pit" is based on testimony presented in Treblinka, written by Jean-Francois Steiner, Translated by Helen Weaver (278).

65.) The historical context of "Love's Mockery" is based on testimony presented in Treblinka, written by Jean-Francois Steiner, Translated by Helen Weaver (308).

66.) The historical context of "Burial" is based on testimony presented in Witnesses to the Holocaust, edited by Rhoda G. Lewin (13).

67.) The historical context of "Camp Games" is based on testimony presented in Witnesses to the Holocaust, edited by Rhoda G. Lewin (64-65).

68.) The historical context of "Bread of Life" is based on testimony presented in Witnesses to the Holocaust, edited by Rhoda G. Lewin (60).

69.) The historical context of "Animal Warmth" is based on testimony presented in Inside the Concentration Camps: Eyewitness Accounts in Hitler's Death Camps, compiled by Eugene Aroneanu, translated by Thomas Whissen (9).

70.) The historical context of "Desolation I" is based on testimony presented in Inside the Concentration Camps: Eyewitness Accounts in Hitler's Death Camps, compiled by Eugene Aroneanu, translated by Thomas Whissen (14).

71.) The historical context of "These Bones Will Shout" is based on testimony presented in Inside the Concentration Camps: Eyewitness Accounts in Hitler's Death Camps, compiled by Eugene Aroneanu, translated by Thomas Whissen (133).

72.) The historical context of "Sterilization" is based on testimony presented in Inside the Concentration Camps: Eyewitness Accounts in Hitler's Death Camps, compiled by Eugene Aroneanu, translated by Thomas Whissen (81).

73.) The historical context of "No Choice" is based on testimony presented in Holocaust Testimonies: The Ruins of Memory, by Lawrence L. Langer (134).

74.) The historical context of "Sisterhood of the Bullet" is based on testimony presented in The Buchenwald Report, translated and edited by David A. Hackett (350).

75.) The historical context of "Punishment" is based on testimony presented in Inside the Concentration Camps: Eyewitness Accounts in Hitler's Death Camps, compiled by Eugene Aroneanu, translated by Thomas Whissen (17).

76.) The historical context of "Because" is based on testimony presented in Witnesses to the Holocaust, edited by Rhoda G. Lewin (82).

77.) The historical context of "Furnace of Life" is based on testimony presented in Witnesses to the Holocaust, edited by Rhoda G. Lewin (89).

78.) The historical context of "Vengeance" is based on testimony presented in Witness: Voices from the Holocaust, edited by Joshua M. Greene and Shiva Kumar (165-66).

79.) The historical context of "Still" is based on testimony presented in Witnesses to the Holocaust, edited by Rhoda G. Lewin (10).

CPSIA information can be obtained at www.ICGtesting.com
Printed in the USA
BVOW07s0141080914

365721BV00002B/73/P